undercurrent

undercurrent

rita wong

WITH DRAWINGS BY CINDY MOCHIZUKI

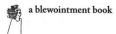 a blewointment book

NIGHTWOOD EDITIONS

2015

Nightwood Editions
P.O. Box 1779, Gibsons, BC, V0N 1V0, Canada
www.nightwoodeditions.com

TYPESETTING & COVER DESIGN: Carleton Wilson
COVER ART: Marika Swan · INTERIOR DRAWINGS: Cindy Mochizuki

Nightwood Editions acknowledges financial support from the Government of Canada through the Canada Book Fund and the Canada Council for the Arts, and from the Province of British Columbia through the British Columbia Arts Council and the Book Publisher's Tax Credit.

This book has been produced on 100% post-consumer recycled, ancient-forest-free paper, processed chlorine-free and printed with vegetable-based dyes.

Printed and bound in Canada.

LIBRARY AND ARCHIVES CANADA CATALOGUING IN PUBLICATION

Wong, Rita, 1968-, author
Undercurrent / Rita Wong ; with drawings by Cindy Mochizuki.

Poems.
"A blewointment book".
Issued in print and electronic formats.
ISBN 978-0-88971-308-6 (pbk.).--ISBN 978-0-88971-045-0 (pdf)

I. Title.

PS8595.O5975U54 2015   C811'.54   C2015-901130-2
                                                 C2015-901131-0

"We do not own the water. The water owns itself."

—Lee Maracle

The water belongs to itself.

"Empty your mind, be formless, shapeless, like water. If you put water into a cup, it becomes the cup. You put water into a bottle, and it becomes the bottle. You put it in a teapot, it becomes the teapot. That water can flow, or it can crash. Be water my friend."

—Bruce Lee

我很感謝這裡的原住民

－黃錦兒

CONTENTS

PACIFIC FLOW

water has a syntax   i am still learning

a middle voice   pivots where it is porous

foraminifera punctuate   ocean floors
salmon streams   double as human & bear lifelines

an underlying platform   marine reclaims its own
from trough to crest   hypersea rolls through meme

tidal rhythm   sings convoluta roscoffensis
silica circuits   iodine invokes thyroid

saltiness grows over eons   plankton provide half our oxygen
what we cannot see   matters as kin

fever speeds us up   churns soluble toxins, insoluble plastics
strikes gulls   spikes trawls

choppy waves warn   hazardous passages
abound from   city sewage

mess amasses   dissonant grammar
wail overfished   bluefins tune

benthic beholds   watches & weights
learning curves   gurgles to the surface

Pacific Ocean's the real boss — Fred Wah

dedicated to The Sea Around Us by Rachel Carson and Sea Sick by Alanna Mitchell

the great pacific garbage patch is not just a mass of
floating plastic junk the size of ontario, jostling
about with jellyfish and starving squids in the
ocean, but a dead albatross mirrors us back to
ourselves. it is a manmade network, toxic magic in
the making, branching into your bathroom with its
plastic shampoo bottles & toothbrushes, into local
plastic factories, into the fast food restaurants that
sing the convenient song & inconvenient truth of
disposable forks & styrofoam containers, into the
plastic beverage bottles belched out by nestle, coca-
cola, pepsi, visible tip of the corporate iceberg. it
is embedded in mutual funds & stock investments.
it is soap dish & lawn chair, eyeglasses & twist ties,
hospital food trays & squeezable honey bottles,
lighters & lipstick tubes, all bobbing & decomposing
in a great big salty home. it is formidable & humble,
far away & intimate, outside & inside, all at once.

THE SEA AROUND US, THE SEA WITHIN US

both the ferned & the furry, the herbaceous &
the human, can call the ocean our ancestor. our
blood plasma sings the composition of seawater.
roughly half a billion years ago, ocean reshaped
some of its currents into fungi, flora & fauna that
left their marine homes & learned to exchange
bodily fluids on land. spreading like succulents
& stinging nettles, our salty-wet bodies refilled
their fluids through an eating that is also always
drinking. hypersea is a story of how we rearrange
our oceanic selves on land. we are liquid matrix,
streaming & recombining through ingesting one
another, as a child swallows a juicy plum, as a beaver
chews on tree, as a hare inhales a patch of moist,
dewy clover. what do we return to the ocean that let
us loose on land? we are animals moving extracted
& excreted minerals into the ocean without plan
or precaution, making dead zones though we are
capable of life.

MONGO MONDO

12 midday at midway, sun glares plastic trashed, beached, busted
bottle caps, broken lighters, brittle shreds in feathered corpses

heralded by the hula hoop & the frisbee, this funky plastic age
spins out unplanned aftermath, ongoing agony

mostly unseen, brilliant in the midst of daylight
polestar shines on, guiding proper motion
tortoise, albatross, crab & dolphin pod
brace against onslaught: how
long will it take the clan to learn?
convenience not worth cancer's
long soft leak into lungs, brains, bellies
distended, grotesque imitations of feeding
hidden hunger can't be satisfied by junk tossed
after one use, to be carried by wind & waves

into random access memory through online photographs
into inhaled weather, ingesting hormone scrambling seafood

trapped in massive ghost nets, angry flails are human, yet won't
    get us out
concerted cutting, strategic to the source, might avert our own
    disposal

"plastic is toxic both to make and to dispose of" — Elizabeth Royte, Garbage Land

THE WONDERS OF BEING SEVERAL

belt a bivocal ditty to honour the micro & the macro
as symbiotic bacteria outnumber our juicy cells ten to one
surrounded & surrounding, we persevere
through this episode called industrialization
among microbiome evolved with skin & lips, maw & gullet
bacteria buddies swim throughout
adapting & absorbing
wiggling & digesting
sugar, protein, fat
the yummy stuff
but furbished with furans
they kick up a fuss
break rank, revoke immunity

broken lines get parsed back into a cycle where
the big eat the small but the small eventually eat the big
humble ends become modest beginnings

thank the great decomposers
quiet multitudes within
as unsettlers excavate like there's no tomorrow
so much short-term gold, long-term arsenic
short-term bitumen, long-term cancer
short-term packaging, long-term polyethylene
for germs to reorganize

"the role of the infinitely small is infinitely large" — Louis Pasteur

14

let the colonial borders be seen for the pretensions that they are
i hereby honour what the flow of water teaches us
the beauty of enough, the path of peace to be savoured
before the extremes of drought and flood overwhelm the careless
water is a sacred bond, embedded in our plump, moist cells
in our breaths that transpire to return to the clouds that gave us
    life through rain
in the rivers & aquifers that we & our neighbours drink
in the oceans that our foremothers came from
a watershed teaches not only humbleness but climate fluency
the languages we need to interpret the sea's rising voice
water connects us to salmon & cedar, whales & workers
its currents bearing the plastic from our fridges & closets
a gyre of karma recirculates, burgeoning body burden
i hereby invoke fluid wisdom to guide us through the toxic muck
i will apprentice myself to creeks & tributaries, groundwater &
    glaciers
listen for the salty pulse within, the blood that recognizes marine
    ancestry
in its chemical composition & intuitive pull
i will learn through immersion, flotation & transformation
as water expands & contracts, i will fit myself to its ever-changing
    dimensions
molecular & spectacular, water will return what we give it, be that
arrogance & poison, reverence & light, ambivalence & respect
let our societies be revived as watersheds

"water is unstoppable" — *Wes Nahanee, from the Squamish Nation*

because i am part of the problem i can also become part of
    the solution

although i am part of the problem i can also become part of
    the solution
where i am part of the problem i need to be part of the solution
while i am part of the problem i can also be part of the solution
one part silt one part clear running water one part blood love
    sweat
not *tar* but *tears*, *e* inserts a listening, witnessing, quickening eye
broken but rebinding, token but reminding, vocal buck
    unwinding
the machine's gears rust in rain, moss & lichen slowly creep life
    back
the rate of reclamation is humble while the rate of destruction
    blasts fast
because we are part of the problem we can also become part of
    the solution

16   *Who are we? We are the beings who need clean water in order to live a life of dignity, joy and good relation. Maybe you are part of "us" without even knowing that you are. Maybe we are the ones who are too often taken for granted or ignored, the quiet witnesses to atrocities, greed, mean-spirited hierarchies, hostages of capitalism. Maybe we are remembering what it means to respect water, because doing so is to respect ourselves, our shared, fluid vulnerability, our funny contradictions, our stumbling, dancing, crying, laughing, eating, drinking, pissing, working, playing, burping, farting, messy selves. Maybe we are the thunderstorms that precipitate when too much has been repressed, the weeds that refuse to stop, the coyotes, the grandmothers, the yet unborn. Maybe we are flash floods, demoralized workers, the hospitalized, the angry entitled children who don't even remember to thank the water that keeps them alive. Maybe we are system change as well as climate change. Dripping & spitting, we rise.*

FRESH ANCIENT GROUND

"Since 1978, over 14 billion dollars
have been taken out of our traditional territory.
Yet my family still goes without running water."
— Melina Laboucan Massimo, Lubicon Cree woman

"When you can't trust the water, it's terrifying"
— James Cameron visiting the tar sands

can the water trust us?

chasing temporary jobs that evaporate
like so much acid rain drifting into Saskatchewan

"overburden removal" leaves poisonous polycyclic aromatic
    hydrocarbons, pah
the PAHs stink — swallow them and die a slow cancerous death

those who don't respect the magic of ice
are doomed to melt it for their descendants

as miles of living medicines made by rivers over millennia
are unceremoniously eradicated, annihilated, wasted

everything leaking everywhere it wasn't meant to go
rainbow in the sky or on slick oil

held captive by toxic water, undrinkable yet thinkable,
blistering fish inside out, thirsty children sickened

caribou killed by omnibus rampage, eliminating water
from legislation in the federal abdication of responsibility

what is the language of decay & how can we not afford to learn
  that dialect?

350, 398, 400, 450 as the outer count changes the inner one

we walk for healing the scar sands, in a living pact with the
  bears, the eagles,
the muzzled scientists, the beavers who've built dams you can
  see from outer space

step by step, we conduct ceremony for those who don't know
any better or don't care, broken whole, waiting for our sisters &
brothers to catch up with wind, sun & water

*From 2010 to 2013, I committed to participate in the Healing Walk for the
Tar Sands, as well as a fifth year helping to organize a solidarity healing walk in
Montreal. I have no words big enough for the horror I feel when I see and smell
the tar sands. Bearing witness to the devastation is one of the hardest things I have
ever done. Alone, I would have curled into a fetal ball and sobbed for what has
been lost and destroyed. Even now, when I think about the land up north, let
myself feel the brutality that has been normalized through massive industry, my
throat stops and my eyes fill with tears. In the company of the healing walkers, led
by indomitable Cree and Dene elders and everyday people, determined Keepers of
the Athabasca, mothers, fathers, aunties, uncles, concerned citizens, we reassert
human responsibilities to land, water, life.*

*These responsibilities can be fostered or ignored by the cultures we are raised in, but
the responsibilities and relationships remain regardless of how we are socialized.
They are embedded in each breath we take, each sip of water we swallow, each bite
of food provided by the land, no matter how much humans manipulate, redirect,
reshape or try to control what the earth provides.*

Whether or not we were taught these responsibilities by our families and education systems, we can still learn how to address them. We can remember that dignity and meaning comes from keeping the earth healthy for future generations for all living creatures, plants and animals, not just humans. We can look frankly at what is not going well—the destruction of natural habitat, the dangers posed by global warming, the inequities and violence in our own cultures—and do better. We are capable of it, if we care to try.

"The destruction of the aquatic ecosystem health of our rivers and streams through poorly considered land use policy is the landscape equivalent of wiping out the immunological capacity of your own blood stream" — Robert Sandford

JOURNEY TO THE WEST 西遊記

20   canoe journeyers are
      coast protecting itself
      where ocean meets rock is home
      when ocean meets oil is poison
      one container crash turns
      fresh sea urchin breakfast
      to wretched carcinogen

      if nothing ever spills, leaks or collides
      (implausible & impossible)
      the burn itself still bankrupts children's lives
      forecloses futures

      earth monkey, girl spirit, one of millions
      whose parents migrated to turtle island
      on this journey to the west
      modestly does what the coast calls us to do
      to protect future monkeys
      even a future for corporations
      depends on guardians
      protecting the coastal home
      that we are part of
      home in the big sense
      ancient as basic stone

"This, I submit, is the freedom of real education, of learning how to be well-adjusted: You get to consciously decide what has meaning and what doesn't." — David Foster Wallace, This is Water

In spring 2014, canoeing in the gentle River of Golden Dreams near Whistler, BC, I fell in when we snagged on a branch and suddenly tipped over. The shock of cold water awoke me into vigilance. Wearing a lifejacket did not eliminate the fear I felt as the river enveloped me completely, reminded me of its power.

Ironically, I cannot swim, though I have taken lessons over the years, and continue to try learning in an on-again, off-again way, as skin and health permit. Having addressed barriers to swimming in the city one by one — finding an ozone-purified pool instead of a chlorinated one, getting prescription goggles, practising kicks, etc. I have improved but still find myself woefully clumsy and tense in the water, as it conducts so much sound and stimulus, thicker than air. How can someone write a book with and for water, and not swim? Very humbly and respectfully, I would say. It's not so much that I fear the water, as I fear my own inability to manoeuvre in it, based in part on my reluctance to relax, the resistance to submit to the water's own dynamics for more than a few breaths. This is partly what I mean when I say that I am still learning water's syntax. I mean that in a much larger way too, though. One water body flows together with other water bodies, a whole greater than its parts: "What you cannot do alone, you will do together."

Thanks to the river's prompting, I will return to the swim lessons when the time and conditions are right. In the meantime, even for those of us who don't swim, water rules! Our cities and lifestyles are built upon it, whether we know it or not. Try going a day, or three, without water. Water gives us life. What do we give back to water?

In summer 2014, I was honoured to read one of Chief Dan George's poems at the Salish Seas Festival, hosted by the Tsleil-Waututh Sacred Trust. In "Words to a Grandchild," he writes, "Each day brings an hour of magic. Listen to it!"

That day, I felt the hour of magic while joining the canoe ceremony held by the Tsleil-Waututh in Burrard Inlet. As poets, we were invited along, and I was excited to participate. I was also terrified because I can't swim. What if I tipped the canoe by accident? What if I didn't pull my weight? As I entered the canoe, I said my name out loud in Cantonese and English, then put my fears aside and focused on paddling, trying to keep time with the dozen or so paddlers on the large ceremonial canoe. The fear was still there, lodged in my body, but I did not give it strength. Instead I paddled hard with my right side, prayed for the water and tried to follow instructions as best I could. The ceremony was mind-blowing, body-tiring, heart-opening and spirit-lifting.

There is still a long way to go in my journey with water, which is also a journey of becoming worthy to live as a guest on these sacred lands of the Coast Salish peoples, but that day taught me the power of what can be accomplished together. Not much in my Albertan education prepared me for that moment of sheer love for the land, waters and life, but luckily, something deeper within, both younger and older at once, recognized the gift of that moment. Immense gratitude to the Tsleil-Waututh Sacred Trust for their generous and courageous leadership.

Gratitude also to Makhabn, known as the Bow River, whose waters kept me alive the first twenty years of my life, & who taught me the power of water from an early age, as it steadily flowed through the City of Calgary where I grew up. That river is what prepared me to love this inlet, other rivers, the ocean.

NIGHT GIFT

make space and let the night speak through you—what will the darkness say?

will it sigh the song of night-cleaners, the lament of the wrongly imprisoned, the rage of the ragged, the dispossessed? how will the night take *you* back? will you be the vessel for earth shatter, hydro poison, ancestral revenge? perhaps steady weeds, growing irrepressibly into the cracks, urban repurposing, straddling both the drugs that kill & the ones that heal? the globe moves around the sun, unstoppable, feeding pine trees & the petro-state alike, giving us the days and nights by which to stand with the trees, what the oil industry calls *overburden,* or to die more rapidly, more stupidly, by peak oil. as rivers & oceans fill with carcinogenic wastes from the petroleum-plastic supply chain, the political systems follow, stuffed full of suncorpse & tired old neocolonial ego that refuses to stop growing until it reaches the limits of the planet's patience. who knows what alliances & monkey wrenches will be enough to stop the greed of the greasy machine? what i do know is the humble migrants who've travelled the ocean have felt its wisdom more deeply than an arrogant elite that doesn't heed the world's necessary stories. jail the stories & the storytellers, but they will keep speaking the night, until empire expires, with or without the multitudes alive. in this race may we be ready to move fast, yet steady enough to encompass musicians & lake gatherings, forests & guerrilla gardens, fuelled by a love more immense than the injustices we've inherited. we need to live the world that is possible even while we struggle through war. respect living coasts & fluid watersheds, not murderous imperial borders. in grief & in celebration, in fear & in courage, in anger & in compassion, the night replenishes us so that we may continue to embody her songs.

"Water is to land what the voice is to the body." — *Kaluli knowledge, via Steven Feld & Walter Lew*

too long a sacrifice can make a toxin of the earth.

o when may it suffice?

—

we burn ancient sunlight & petrified ancestors
like there's no tomorrow
dig & draw up dirt so relentlessly we tip toward stranglehold
does capitalism's "progress" induce collapse?
ed said, "everything's been touched by oil"
i look through plastic glasses caught under
petroleum by-product lenses
first unwitting then unwilling recipient of
profit-seeking pillage sickening scale
stunned with eerie disquiet escalating horror pulses
carcinogens every which way
brutal menace monstrous crime scene
poison & violence leaking
into the Athabasca river to the fast-melting Arctic
systemic amnesia operates on the earth's forest green skin
cuts out life with detached, sociopathic precision,
overburdens pines & birches
dead ducks, canaries in the coal mine, turgid trout,
delusional destruction spreads out
explosive & erosive, manufactured discontent digs for
more, more, more
mammoth gashes extracted till abandoned
like so many arrogant american swimming pools in the desert
or chinese dams big enough to make the planet tremble for days
imperial delirium's race to the bottom
at the expense of the watchers
an expanse of hidden relations disregarded for distraction,

an immature culture pumped
on blunt ambition, hydrocarbon hubris,
such malignant pustules to be
shrugged off by intensifying storms & quakes
banal tyranny, drunk-on-god trick, devastating heists from
the banks of the river scarring the earth
scaring the unborn who hover, wondering what meets them

upon seeing her capture reflected within burtynsky's photos,
     the hostage of the petro-state
renders a diagnosis of stockholm syndrome, self-administers
     the necessary remedies
so terribly simple, so utterly unachieved so far:
to kick the oil addiction for love of water
to inhabit the earth with the dignity owed to life-giving dirt
to fulfill our responsibilities chthonic & cosmic
to make a story large enough, generous enough to become
     better neighbours
with the winged, the finned, the four-legged, the stumbling
     two-leggeds
another world is not only possible, she is already here, carrying
     on underneath our feet
reconstituting us with each new sip of ancient water
reassembling us into the sacred headwater's continuum
so we can aspire to a wiser, wider story, felt in the elders'
     strong, calm hands raised in Iskut,
Klabona Keepers hold our fate in the courage to say *enough*
witness this ghastly corporate moment striving to mature into
     great return
a blessed unrest like three-thousand-year-old rice paddies
     mirroring our stars back to us
reminding us to live within the budget of what the sun
     abundantly provides each day
meridians align to rebalance what's vital,
downstream living bodies
countless geese flocking overhead, wind-swayed cottonwood,
     magical caribou, garrulous groundhogs, handcuffed
     grannies, plentiful plankton, playful nieces, spawning
     salmon, song-rich mothers, mountain goats, resolute
     swanning, steady sheep, eagle soar, autonomous aunties,

hemlock, wolf howl, venerable moose, grizzly bears, swift
horses, nimble nephews, humble fathers, blessed cedar,
spawning char, steady swimmers, storytellers, rivers
devotedly rising from the unceded earth against systems of mass
    destruction
committing to the union of the living
a current of spacious canoes propelling renewal with each
    stroke
a murmuration of ancestors and descendants soaring forth
where the poison is found, look for the cure nearby,
    honouring sacred debts all the time
how do we give back more than we have taken?
what better gifts can we offer?
kindred spirit, autonomous water remembers
forest before rubble
revives the forest after the terror is reined in

A MAGICAL DICTIONARY FROM BITUMEN
TO SUNLIGHT

cadence   : the sound of one material meeting another,
            hello!
          : heartbeat, disrupted & adapting
          : tree percussion, funky fir cavitation

crushed   : pressing so hard as to lose one's own shape
          : tiny privatized homes the size of skulls
            or microchips relying on rare earth across
            continents
          : what capitalism has executed upon forests

ancestors : holding my body up through cellular memory,
            anonymous
          : condensed over eons into mineral wealth
          : material in the headlights, reconfigured as a
            vintage car more retro than we know,
            heavy metals millennia old

carries   : one act of the written word
          : a sapling song courtesy of xylem, transpires to
            proliferate in the ether

ceremony : shaping one's gestures to honour what has not
            been lost, just buried
          : the music that we forget is music

mercurial : a host of premonitions, close to the source
          : the sound of fire in the sky

micro   : a power we don't have words for
             : the burgess shale in your eyelashes

bitumen   : buried ancestors, unearthed & burned to expand
                 the ocean
             : pitched sacrifice zone wherever it bubbles up,
                 hellishly excavated

sunlight   : in orchestra with monthly pull, nocturnal howl
             : beaming in the future, a planetary revolution, a
                 graced turning

祖先

REMEMBERING THE FUTURE

30   a circular muscle, tubular imperative, propels internal
       concoctions

a transit from warm inner mulch to outer lucency burbles

as traffic empties its gasoline chambers into the atmosphere

expanding into gas eight times its liquid weight

mutual promise unmet though embedded within our
       compromised states

daily peristalsis regular & rhythmic

rates of flow through my riverbank body

every highway putting out the fire with gasoline

volatility standards lowered in a race to the bought-out

hedging bets in the midst of a photochemical frenzy

the bottom line, the one on which we all traverse, is as free

as the quiet air you breathe

horse & sail more prescient than passé

in an abundance of sun, wind, absorbent, acidifying,
       expanding ocean

skeletal starfish quiver, melt & pulse scrotal with emissions

many-chambered hearts, one-chambered sky

behold a dizzying ballad of reckless express

until quiet & beauty return to the land

"[The Zapatista] revolution spirals outward and backward, away from some of the colossal mistakes of capitalism's savage alienation, industrialism's regimentation, and toward old ways and small things; it also spirals inward via new words and new thoughts." — Rebecca Solnit

immersed in chlorinated water
immersed in formaldehyde off-gas
immersed in car exhaust
immersed in the oxygen produced by oceanic plankton
immersed in windy chinook
immersed in barbecue aroma
immersed in smog
immersed in someone's sneeze
immersed in the oxygen produced by cedar
immersed in the oxygen produced by fir
immersed in the oxygen produced by hemlock
immersed in carbon dioxide
immersed in the colonial present
immersed in loonsong
immersed in endocrine disrupting dust
immersed in the smell of the ocean
immersed in stale air
immersed in English
immersed in ego-jacking capitalism
immersed in thought
immersed in ancestral respect, or not
immersed in natureculture
immersed in electromagnetic fields
immersed in gravity
immersed in radio waves
immersed in multilingual contact zone
immersed in transmission frequencies
immersed in ultraviolet rays
immersed in someone's perfume
immersed in ambient sound
immersed in neighbourhood vibe

immersed in urban hurry
immersed in pedestrian drift
immersed in the protocol of sunlight
immersed in the irrepressible commons, come on!
immersed in q'élstexw

The forest is falling.
It hears itself.
The rain ineluctable
Speechless and necessary.
– Phyllis Webb

UNSUNG SERVICE

for Staləw, the Fraser River

perched on a paddlewheeler, typing on my fraught laptop
on the *Samson V*, in the midst of freshet
big puppy-eyed, sleek river otter silently glides.
together otter & i witness raw logs floating down the Fraser
accelerated export to empires south & east of us
quickly doubling sales of tree kill, when we, the moose & the
    murrelets want
the trees here, alive
tree care is self-care
ship's whistle blasts, deep & foggy
once manned by Captain Drinkwater, trans *Samson* calls
shallow, steady & strong, she faces the port where mazdas &
    audis enter
as raw logs exit, the engine of capitalist ideology attacks the river
constant container activity as swallows zip, seagulls dive
ladybug, bee, placid mandarin ducks, humans promenade
flip through *Meteorology for Seamen* & *The Theory and Practice of*
    Seamanship on the desk
where does the museum exhibit begin & end?
what will future earthlings find in the neoliberal middens left
    behind?
microbial murmur: tardy but still need to act up
zoanosis prompts
crossing thresholds, game-changers on elder river
footsteps above, creosote beside & interference below
industrial habit morphs fish home into trade zone
underneath the opaque river, life i cannot see
implacable sturgeon carries on
in the river that brought us all here to this city
the river that holds our future in its flows

"Rivers 'think' round; humans looking at them think straight." — *Christopher Armstrong et al.*

We are tardigrades and tawny owls, river dolphins and rockhopper penguins, slow sloths and fast elk. We are not stuffed animals to be deserted and betrayed as your political "leaders" listen to money and ignore the acidifying ocean, the tumultuous tsunami, hurricanes, floods that shout climate instability. We are your relatives. When you capture us in zoos, you diminish yourselves and us. We precede and supersede Moloch, the Koch brothers and the patriarchal mind games that have been shoved down our throats and into our gall bladders. Some of us will survive you and some of us have not. We call upon you to remember your ancient oaths, your debts to all realms that enable your existence, your obligations as earth-dwellers.

horsetail hints
at abundant water beneath
transformed into fine green nodes

sprouting up from cracks in pavement
near Main & Broadway .
atop what was once Brewery Creek
horsetail hails the sturdy spore, the perpetual wind
its ally in propagation

scrub brush, toothbrush, remover of toxins
horsetail ever-so-slowly heals inflictions
a living fossil who quietly outlasts our cities
soaking up the acid soil we leave behind

二

lavender blossoms
in the traffic circle
guerrilla garden tenacity
fed by rain, sun, evolving bylaws
car exhaust & pedestrian breadth
big doggie breath, small doggie do
fed by kiddy bustle
sensible cyclists balance
loaves of bread in their baskets
buddies play Jimi Hendrix
their guitars kiss the sky
healers turn buds into
salve, tea, soap, story
elementary activity
primary activity
an East Van dance
a black soil miracle
reassuring windsway
contingent cousin
roundabout whiff
soothing the city
one modest root
by mythic root
surviving with
bee by living bee

三

38

found in fields from Halifax to Vancouver
plantain's nickname is white man's footprint
for the way it gets everywhere
yet there is also native plantain
to poultice your cuts & rashes
to heal the sores of everyday life
plantain sits & spreads
mown down & ever growing
overlooked neighbour
gently toughing us all out

四

salal remembers the forests
before the streets
its juicy leaves & tender berries
hold Salish history from the sun
tickled with glistening rains
bolstered with the languorous weight of summer heat
salal ripens

五

after eighty destructive years
industrial blockage of salmon habitat
we celebrate this uncanny return in the city:
salmon to Still Creek in 2012
alert, adept swimmers
kindle, perpetuate, astound
with sleek scaly stamina
miraculous as the salmon that grace Musqueam Creek
with each year's turn around the sun
an unbroken vow between relatives

bone, tendon, muscle, joint inflamed
knuckle, wrinkle, nail, ten half moons
a seven-pound skin, well distributed
so light i don't feel what i carry
rashes, scars, bruises, faint scratches
eczema reminds
fragile barrier, easily broken
inner oozes out, itchy lymph
fluids that came from
swallowed water
that came from
a river that came from a lake
that came from a glacier
receding from industrial glare
pulse quickens
shoulder tenses
sorrow deepens
send signals down spine
fourteen facial bones adapt
mandible stretches, maw yawns
eyes float in moist sockets
while body sweats
& sweats, porous
ongoing experiment
rich in nurdles
poor in ecological literacy
atrazine in your armpits?
pcbs in your pelvic core?
furans in your feet?
dioxins in your diaphragm?
cells burst a chorus
a need for reprieve

A MOVING TARGET

iron, carbon, nitrogen flow
oscillate, oxidize, optimize
cellular symphony
perennially sheds, regenerates
walking mineral body
a watery deposit
chemical composition
shared with the pacific
kuroshio current within
dark salt, sunlit
benthic bowels
a family forest of microfauna
digesting come what may
but thyroid's receptors confused
by polycylic pollution
getting mixed signals
hyper or hypo
as plasticizers slide into
sulfur, magnesium, phosphates
calcium carbonate
an orchestra of nutrients
infiltrated by capital's loud shout
consumed while consuming
disoriented in proprioceptive profusion
seepage from decomposing bottle not just
plastic but democracy degrading
inner monster muscles up
as daily toxins come & go
a revolving door
heads & shoulders
knees & toes
nose & mouth

"What we drink, inhale and find to eat in
the environment external to ourselves
quickly becomes our internal environment"
— Sandra Steingraber

雨

awaken to the gently unstoppable rush of rain landing on roofs, pavement, trees, porches, cars, balconies, yards, windows, doors, pedestrians, bridges, beaches, mountains, the patter of millions of small drops making contact everywhere, enveloping the city in a sheen of wet life, multiple gifts from the clouds, pooled over centuries and channelled to power us, rain propels our water-based bodies that eat other water-based bodies, mineral vegetable animal. when i turn on the shower, i turn my face and shoulders toward post-chlorinated rain. the tap releases free rain to slake our thirst, transformed through pipes and reservoirs. anonymous agent of all that we, unwitting beneficiaries, do. refusing the inertia of amnesia, i welcome the memory of rain sliding into sink and teacup, throat and bladder, tub and toilet. bountiful abundant carrier of what everyone emits into the clouds, be that exhale or smoke, belch or chemical combustion, flame or fragrance, the rain gives it all back to us in spates, a familiar sound, an increasingly mysterious substance

"The rain surrounded the cabin...with a whole world of meaning, of secrecy, of silence, of rumor. Think of it: all that speech pouring down, selling nothing, judging nobody, drenching the thick mulch of dead leaves, soaking the trees, filling the gullies and crannies of the wood with water, washing out the places where men have stripped the hillside... Nobody started it, nobody is going to stop it. It will talk as long as it wants, the rain. As long as it talks I am going to listen." — Thomas Merton

POUNCE

cloud meets retina
smell the air, wait for rain
iris refreshens with
full-moon maple
oceanic inhale
ducks dunk & quack
a migrating comedy
crows cuss & crap
badass neighbours
scouting the scene, the grime
alleyway moss
quiet lichen witness
this northern limit for the loquat
creeping up
skunk home, coyote cranny
teenage wasteland where
grannies sift through dumpsters
rebraiding scraps & sense
mizzle moistens sidewalk & skin
feather & fur
stubborn feral patience beneath
delicious tulip tree
plantain leaf persists

My heart under your foot, sister of a stone. —*Sylvia Plath*

sienna soaks in footsteps
of rubber rainboots
a light muck glistens
beneath the breezeway
arbutus bright, mud heavy

POLLUTION DODGED?

relocated, lodged

in moist fleshy folds

sweating a bullet

up & down thyroid glands

through veins of discontent

discombobulated frenemy

dispersed histories
bioaccumulate

returning in media res ICYMI

bloodstream's poisoned gift

giving & giving & giving

long after the plastic wrap's

chucked in the landfill

trapped in economies

of scale, built on porous shale

see & do? unseen & undone

tweeting up a storm with
intersex bass

riding the toxic rollercoaster

techno treadmill trouncing

underneath skin acting up

while eyes stay on the screen

                      that gets smaller & smaller

        faster & faster

                      for the converted

      & those held hostage

                      as filter bubbles pop

as the mines dug up outside

                      land inside body capsule

    hormonal hurts releasing

                      tricks of the global trade

    my endocrine disruption

                      for your muted phone

          your cancer

                      for my keyboard

  a slow release traffic jam

                      embedded each thin-skinned
                      body

beside the jewelled transmission
                tower

                      a grenade

bisphenol ache bursts a cell wall leaks plasma limpid, laden with toxic gifts courtesy of duped ontology   corporate cancer embedded in diets, morsel by muscle, blight by bite, gradually accumulated illnesses blossom in our bellies, breasts, bladders, intestines testify to trace amounts hoarded in blood & bitumen, brimming with slow malignant release, remind us that biology is determined by chemistry cartels infiltrating our shampoos & synthetic textiles, room deodorizers & tin can linings   receipt paper coatings & hand sanitizers sing a slow song of poison by a thousand exposures

calm in chronic pollution, kindred water is a secret player reflecting industrial flaws back to us. naming the chemical creep is the first step in returning to our responsibilities, finding that duty itself is a ragged, fierce beauty, not just listing the toxins but disrupting their supply chain as we turn our gaze to how they seep intimately, expertly, into the creases we didn't know we had, into our cracked lips & sweating armpits, moistening our dry eyes and callused heels. there is no substitute for earth's authority, the living law of each inhale, each exhale, the quiet dignity of shared breath, necessary balance.

We are undercurrent, overburden, the rolling earth, the spin that won't be doctored, the healers who want to live well on this revolving planet. Our needs are few and our desires many. We need clean water. We need clean air. We need to eat plants powered by sunlight and earth. We need kinship that builds peaceful relations. We need to respect our differences without letting them kill, destroy, displace, incarcerate and oppress us. We need the small picture and the big picture. We need to share. We want to share. We see that obscene wealth for a few is not merely a sign of merit or talent or ability, but also a spiritual sickness, a bloated ego, a reduced capacity to respond to the suffering of one's kin. We want everyone to understand that the tumours in the moose and whitefish and our neighbours are a sign of our failures, not our successes. We are tired of glorifications of war and the reenactments of its impoverished logic in our bureaucracies. We want to restore balance, right relations, ethical being. We cannot afford delusional hierarchies. We will not race each other to the bottom. We commit to live up to the future's call. We want our lives to not be wasted.

tractor with gas pedal for brake
rocks shovel rare earth selenium
titanium reinforces dead worms
dendritic fracked shale hydrogen
sulfide muds water steel caked urge
broken earth torn hole caterpillar
rubble silent rain atrazine spring
dirt dirge drip naphthalene
hydrochloric acid ammonia
benzene formaldehyde xylene
atrazine puddle DDT remnants
tree roots tree corpse petrified
beetle decomposed dinosaur
layers of ancestor bird bones
wolf scat slow water transform
old meat dead petals scattered
pollen bee legs pine memory rich
earth trickle groundwater house
foundations broken grandmother
old crow bark dust landfill moraine
millennial circuit current stream
holocene anthropocene morass
mangle hair cracked femur turned
dirt worms clay salt silt powder
bedrock shale forest corpse oil
burden beast beauty ferny mass
turned black depth night soil human
toil trinkets fish bones clam shells
midden not wasted topsoil air sun
photosynthesis over centuries old
jugs sheaves wheat compacted
earth ancestor owl dried blood
magma gravity packed stone water

FLASH MEMORY

grassy knoll water-carved valley
ice-scratched dip glacial deposit
pebble sand silt dirt accumulation
wet accretion wind-blown layer
packed deep rain sink storm trace
cloud release catchment tree debris
root tangle great-great-great-grandmother's
hair turned soil protein turned nitrogen
phosphorus magnesium clay carbon
history cousin bone disintegration
beetle rebuild worm transformation
micro eats macro makes hummock
grows beans coal extraction burns
plankton corpses dries groundwater
rain replenishes as withdrawals
accelerate competing rates immerse
and deplete the wonder worms wield
thin inches of earth skin soil
on which to perch grow food
reorganize molecules mastodon
robin crow bear beaver hide
buried in transformed by dirt
millennial dirt eons coexist beneath

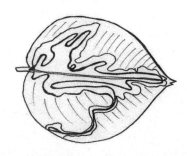

NORTH SHORE SEWAGE STORY

crows party
at the wastewater treatment plant
hop, skip, skim the scum
for meaty delectables
released from urban drains

crows swoop
the bubbling froth
with the grace of gravity

one lone monkey puzzle tree
sits at the lions gate
witnesses sludge stream
gas flares

the huge digesters process
what we have left behind
our discards sifted
chlorinated, pumped out
into the burrard inlet

primary treatment
was built to handle good shit, not
phthalates & flame retardants
birth control pills & antidepressants
morphing fish anatomy
decreasing sperm counts
infiltrating fishy homes

while i long for tertiary rescue
the crows salvage
what they can
from cities industriously pumping out
chemical consequences
transgendering water & children
testing ocean temper

"The era of flush-and-forget is ending... it is the responsibility of every citizen to make sure that defecation means fertilization of the land that feeds us" — Peter Warshall, Septic Tank Practices

LUPUS, A DOUBLED BEING

who teaches the price that "progress" extracts
from our bodies' immune systems
from the seeds of empire
come the dangerous fruit of empire
born on wind & wave
by air & by sea
tempered by kidneys' confusion
filtering the truck of steamships, containers
precious cargo is double-edged, sore with steady emissions
stolen from the source, from underground chambers
taken in industrial mission & precision
mechanical, predictable, implacable onslaught
fist grasp? out slips anorexia, pleonexia
the unrelenting refrain of more, more, more
can subside or crash on our shores
the left brain knows but doesn't believe
in limits to earth's skin, the sacred cave's bonds
the right brain believes but doesn't know
how to stop the lemmings' fall, mass filicide
disney-manufactured in white wilderness, alberta
fiction is flashier than truth, a plastic-signed detour
exported by pipelines, tankers, digital propaganda
that forgets & even sells the ground holding it up
caveat emptor in temporary transaction, transition
to be shed like a stiff vinyl coat that no longer fits
& doesn't breathe. if or when sun-fed cedar
provides a cleaner home, a quiet trail, once overlooked
but returned to through cancer's call, earth's quake
a ring of fire that burns through freeways for
sacrifice or spacious sanctuary

somewhere, a wild swimming wolf looks on

52

We are wet premonition, ferocious spirit waiting for the master's dams to crack, the inexorable and unrepentant rain, the tidal waves taller than tankers, the vigilant survivors of neoliberal snakepits and slimy advertorials. We are the ones who cannot be bought, the ones who will not sell out, the ones who refuse to be bullied, the damp, trembling ones who feel fear in the face of intimidation tactics and propaganda, yet act or bide our time with courage. We will not drink the patented chemical-laced Kool-Aid because we love the taste of spring tap water. We refuse the leaking plastics and insulting poisons that threaten our beloved rivers and oceans. We are freshwater & saltwater, blood & bone, liver & gall bladder, intestinal fortitude, without borders, without names. We are your very breath, the ancestral memory you inhale and the promises you exhale. We are the protocol of life, the Council of All Beings. We are your mother's cervix, your cousin's ulcers, your wake up call after one too many corporate lies insolently or obliviously proclaimed.

54   whose orange tree
        whose window
        whose bedroom
        whose hearth

                            submerged beneath

dam
        three gorges
                            dammed
        yangtze
                    cursed, hearsed
            unless the baiji return

whose shack by the side of the road
                    resists baseline drift

who travels an hour by bus
to reach the empty bank

        who knows the why in wise

            who speaks earth
                    through water

秉愛   白鱀

*"Now the problems have gotten to the point where the
government is unable to continue covering up the issues"*
- Dai Qing

56   cast into the well that endures blood ambush
      encampments, walled cities, whole empires rise & fall
      the well reclaims the depths, nourishes moon and pig

      the town may be changed, thieves, toil, transitory
      but the well cannot be changed

      architecture inexhaustible, abundance
      wheel gentle, gradual, honest, simple, subtle

      ineffectual, careless, disastrous
      ditches, bent and straightened

      a breaking of the jug
      sudden collapse, neglect

      trigram exhorts organism, grey-haired, broad forehead
      parts co-operate for the benefit of the whole

      swampy lowlands, submerged in mud
      calculated waiting, white of the eye, shifting thigh

      deep heavens in the waters:
      thunderclouds, stumbling horse, wrecked chariot
      odor to the far shore

      dangling, submit to
      apprehension & anticipation
      long, high, advance and retreat,
      in its own time close to the grain

strength within, danger in front. midwinter pit, chasm.

strength in the face of danger does not plunge ahead but bides
   its time
whereas weakness in the face of danger grows agitated, has not
   the patience to wait

perseverance brings good fortune
it furthers one to cross the great water

a light will develop out of events
clouds rise up to heaven: hardwood joyous and of good cheer

it will rain. we're ready. persistent, ear[*]

[*] poem generated from found language at http://www.ichingonline.net/

"a compact area of glaciers not much larger than Italy provides the headwaters for the Salween,
the Mekong, the Brahmaputra, the Yellow, the Yangtze — and the Ganges. One human in three
lives downstream — and that's why they live there. Without those rivers, life would be impossible"
— Bill McKibben, "A World that Works," Written in Water

58   dreaming of a red chamber she is stranded from her blood's rice
paddies spewing sick roses & smokestacks instead of couplets &
odes to guava   harvest tilapia cultivation pomelo promise
the day is as long as the shore of the continent   sometimes she
cries without knowing which affront in the rampage marketed
as progress, or which unstoppable grace powered by the sun,
caused it   the throat's fullness, the heart's hesitation, remind
her that intuition is a wild horse   struck by constant itch in
the invisible night   she has never seen waters so clear & lucid
before   scratch the surface & meridians abound underneath
linking foot, ear, heart, liver in the body's complex orchestra
accompanied & enabled by spirochetes & microflora   the
channels of return are unpredictable   they follow the paths of
dreamtime that evaporate with sunrise   she is held in a moon
chamber   clouds recharge
the distant hills   she hears amanda nahanee tell the story
wild rice used to grow where chinatown is now   she
invokes its return

                                      q'élstexw

Q'ÉLSTEXW

the city paved over with ~~cement~~ *english cracks open, stubborn* Halq'eméylem
springs up

among the newspaper boxes and mail receptacles in the shade of the thqa:t

along the sidewalks lined with grass and pta:kwem *waiting to grow anywhere
they can*

around the supermarkets full of transported food — kwukemels, *tomatoes,
chocolate and chicken.*

under the wet green shelter of chestnut and p'xwelhp *leaves*

carried on the tricky wings of skwówéls, *also known as* qukin, gaak,
gwawis, setsé7 *and more in the languages of this land*

more to tree & bracken & cucumber & oak & raven than meets the stiff I
root & stomach & seed speak glottal, gut & gift

return

* Halq'eméylem, Ktunaxa, Gitsenimx, Nisgaa, Kwakwala, and Secwepemc
words from http://www.firstvoices.com

60
sewage wafts up at the corner of fifth and st. george
slosh gurgle downhill through indifferent pipe grid pipe grind
your teeth pipe miles and miles of pipe underneath our feet

smell water rushing under the manhole covers
one pipe carries drinking water
another carries away your toilet flush
pipe down, pipe plastic, pipe slime, pipe
time

corner the hydrant bursts chlorinated
water shoots exuberant into sky

coincidence, haunting, or the stubborn stream's refusal to be
confined?

what's lost? not just the streams but the people
who stole them from the salmon who swam them

re-pair tributary with daylight
twin riparian zone with home

detourne st. george toward chief dan george
Geswanouth Slahoot's spirit knows these unceded streams
Snauq Staulk, te Statləw

地下水

"Lower frequencies are the mind / What happened to the creek / Is what happened/ to the sentence
in the twentieth century / It got social underground ///you should make yourself uncomfortable /
If not you who" — Brenda Hillman, Practical Water

alpha bets, language gambles, on

                              land

                                        asks, what're you so
                                        scared of identity for?   61
it's like being scared to say, you're a blade of grass
                                        in a lawn that's
                                        gonna get mowed

declare yourself or not, you'll get cut down & grow back, cut
     down & grow back,
cut down & erode
in the colonial rut

                         unless you ask hey, who imposed these
                         lawns & do i really
want them?

                         traded for forests & prairies & organic
                         garden
futures

the big combine's coming on down, petroleum products
chugging into our lungs & people with many names or no names
gotta keep in mind the ground underneath is what really feeds us
                              the ground was stolen
                                   through lies, deceit, conceit:
                         how does one handle two, three, four-
                         faced adversaries?
the tricks
          with the knife
                         i'm learning to do:
                                        splice languages
                                        barter carefully
call it gaia or gravity,
                    respect the land, mother's worth

seek shelter in meditation bowling community gardening
farmers' market friends meeting conversing in boisterous
classroom reading library quiet stretching yoga's studio inhale

rumpling sleepwarm bed exhale squeezing hotly crowding leafy
park smelling salal patch resting futon firmly soft armchair
beach banyan tree coral reef cafe aerobics working out

bicycle riding kayaking verbing kitchen laundry poncho shawl
hugging howling powwowing concerting guitar spa deli choir
artist-run centre nightclub dojo theatre bar pavilion patio

porch alley stairwell balcony corridor campus chatting room
naturopathic clinic scooping litchi ice cream picnicking jazzing
festival kissing slow nuzzling quick independent bookstore

dictionary sutra swallowing water tasting honey sitting restaurant
walking-in closet study window sill rice cooker curbside walkway
salty-wet dreaming rubbing gently promenading

midnight mountain hiking rendez-vous lovers' arming parade
overhang bus stop video projector strike annual general meeting
quilting bee potluck cooler hamper basket

community centre gymnasium hostel tending orchard grove
cookbook riding train sauntering flip flops muumuu miso bowl
wok night market skeining wool peeling pomelo

hot empanada warm bannock flipping magazine anthology
entering subway salad teahouse feast house longhouse bathtub
pounding piano braiding hair opening thermos plantain

poultice diving into stew lake campsite well unfolding secrets
sketchpad notebook creek

"We embody the hydrological cycle, but this is not a cycle of mere addition and subtraction. Rather, it is a cycle of continuous becoming and transformation."

— Astrida Neimanis, "We Are All Bodies of Water"

i live at the west entrance of a haunted house called canada
whose hungry ghosts, windborn spirits, call us to conscience

when the truth & reconciliation commission arrived
thanks to the concurrent exhibition, *net–eth: going out of the darkness*
i heard the story of a local artist, a survivor of the residential
    schools,
who earlier in his life used bullets as lead to draw his art
another artist pointed out that her family's healing time is
    different from the TRC's schedule

when i walk the path of the rainway in my neighbourhood, as i
    did today
i feel the quick press of clock time, monkey mind
the slow depth of stream time, gut strong
the push pull of moon earth, street sky

an imperfect dance can still bring together
the broken, the dead, the scared & the scabbed, the makers
    & remakers
the children, the elders, the families, the storytellers, the
    witnesses

we walk this path, aching to heal, somehow
dirtied hands, stumbling feet, agile hearts, determined faces
knowing that reconciliation needs land restoration to ground
    itself & grow

sometimes faltering yet steadily recovering, we lean into this
    necessity
rising from the watersheds we become together when we drink
    from them
underneath all the words, we are one troubled water, learning
    to heal ourself

☰

Close to its headwaters, Staləw, otherwise known as the Fraser River, is clear translucent jade, liquid magic.

Fraser Crossing is the farthest point along the Fraser River that one can reach easily by car, without taking a day's hike into the Rocky Mountains. I went there on a trip to pay my respects to staləw, which, in its ceaseless flow for roughly twelve million years, has created the landscape on which I live, otherwise known as Vancouver.

At Fraser Crossing, what I found, in addition to the beautiful, burgeoning river, shocked me: a high-pressure petroleum pipeline had been built underneath the river.

There in the so-called "protected wilderness" of Mount Robson Provincial Park, the Trans Mountain Pipeline has already been very busy. In fact, the old 24"-diameter pipeline has been joined by a new 30"- to 36"-diameter pipeline alongside it, accelerating the extraction of oil from the tar sands. The expanded pipeline runs from Hinton, AB to Tete Jaune Cache, BC.

What the river taught me on this trip is that it is in danger from petroleum.

三

travelling with the stalwart Keepers of the Athabasca
we go to learn, to fulfill our responsibilities together
where wild cranberries, blueberries, labrador tea
grow together in the bush alongside five lakes
and a pond of healing waters
at the 2011 Keepers of the Water gathering
hosted by the Northlands Dene First Nation
a small community of less than a thousand Dene people
with huge hospitality, kindness, care
generously welcomed us with bannock and stew
we feasted on campfire caribou and juicy trout
elders spoke of surviving hydro dam destruction,
tar sands, uranium mines, global warming
the need for unity and action
love for sacred water
curious children came, asked questions
an elder said, when i speak of water, i don't mean
the rivers and lakes, i mean the women

women are water, yes

四

Former World Bank Vice President Ismail Serageldin famously
said that future wars will be fought over water, in the way they're
being fought over oil today. Wars are already being fought over
water, in that water scarcity intensifies existing tensions that we
might perceive as political or religious from an androcentric
lens. But water also presents both an opportunity and a
requirement for communities to work together to protect it, and
in so doing to simultaneously honour ourselves, our relations to

one another. As such, it forms a critical nexus through which to reimagine ourselves and our cultures.

By contemplating the relations and interdependencies that are enacted through water, we can participate in water ethics, walk an inviting path to peace, a way to rethink and address the conflicts and injustices that logically arise when water is conceptualized as an object and commodity to be transported and sold to whichever customer can afford to pay. Grasp it, and it slips through your fingers. Share it wisely, and your communities prosper. Water is our living connector, a gentle yet powerful way to be in relation to one another.

"Let's not mistake capitalism for democracy." — George Soros

"Is the economy serving us or are we serving the economy?" — Radha D'Souza

FOR GREGOIRE LAKE   *which way does the wind blow?*

68

our tents are ready to sleep in   *360*
when we arrive in the dark, tired   *lead*
having made hundreds of sandwiches   *mercury*
for the Healing Walk   *cadmium*

in the fresh morning   *hexavalent chromium*
i dip my hands into you tentatively   *arsenic*
thankful to camp on your shores   *aluminum*
amidst mosquitoes, mud & grass   *zinc*
knowing you hold airborne toxins   *thallium*
from the tar sands   *nickel*

though you look placid, peaceful   *dibenzothiophenes*
you hold bitter, bitumized depths   *phenanthrenes*
protracted violence has been done to you   *fluoranthenes*
to your fish, your birds, your dwellers   *benzanthracenes*

a lake is surrounded   *anthracenes*
though not usually in this way   *pyrenes*
i wish i had met you in better times   *chrysenes*
but i am grateful to meet you at all   *trace metals*

even in our compromised states   *antimony*
we remember why we are here   *365*

*NOTE: Terms on the right are drawn from *Evaluation of Four Reports on
Contamination of the Athabasca River System by Oil Sands Operations*, prepared
for the Government of Alberta, 2011

"Water is life. Oil is money." — Francois Paulette

catastrophic world records—biggest landfill, largest nuclear meltdown, most voracious corporation, most toxic tailings pond, most brutal massacre, hottest year, most rapid species extinction—collapse of easter island, vikings died out on greenland while the inuit survived, global economy's spectre—choose your direction/devotion carefully

trophic cascade, phytoplankton, unravelling circuit boards, algae, jellyfish, crows, cockroaches, viruses, bacteria, endocrine disrupters, acid rain, technicians of the inadvertent, old rags, rascals, spools of tape, dusty boxes, the dark nurse, grains, husks and shatter, how quietly this night releases our cumulative monuments to ourselves

70   the big sacred fire burns, night & day,
         despite the radioactive waste leaked by
         dada-thay, Dene for "death rock," uranium

         open-eared, open-hearted
         i arrive in Wollaston Lake
         home of the Hatchet Lake Denesuline
         walk lightly, gratefully, here on the edge of
         Saskatchewan's biggest lake
         one of its hundred thousand lakes
         overlooked & underestimated
         by those down south
         who desecrate the water for the mines

         further north
         a village of widows
         mourn husbands
         lost to the brutal industry
         for atomic warfare
         they understand responsibility
         when western governments don't—
         they apologize to the survivors
         of Hiroshima
         & Nagasaki for death
         rock taken from their homelands
         without knowledge
         of the consequences

further south
cancer-ridden Navajo
with over 1300 abandoned
dada-thay mines
refuse to allow any more
death rock mining
on their homelands

in contrast to Saskatchewan
the Saudi Arabia of uranium mining
digging & burning up
what rightfully belongs to the future
leaking its deadly mess
into our nervous, drenched bodies

In 1985, roughly two hundred Indigenous people and their allies blocked traffic in and out of Rabbit Lake (now the world's second largest uranium mine) and Collins Bay, documented in Miles Goldstick's book, Wollaston. Canada is one of the world's largest exporters of uranium, due to northern Saskatchewan, epicentre of the mining. Because uranium radiation is silent, invisible, without taste or smell, its carcinogenic effects may not be immediately apparent, but take time to unfold in people and animals.

In August 2010, I participated in the Keepers of the Water IV Conference in Wollaston Lake, northern Saskatchewan. This remote community can only be reached by barge/boat or airplane as there are no roads that go directly there. People say that the water is clean enough there that you can drink it right out of the lake, which I saw people doing. Wollaston Lake is the largest of the hundred thousand lakes that sit within Saskatchewan's boundaries.

Generously hosted by the Hatchet Lake Denesuline First Nation, the conference structure was as fluid as the topic of water itself. A one-hour elder's panel on the conference schedule spontaneously expanded into over eight and a half hours of testimony over two days, as twenty-three elders spoke movingly of how important water is, how cancer caused by mining has killed many family members, how uranium mining and tar sands expansion is poisoning the land. Any elder who wanted to speak was given time, and the way the telling unfolded was an excellent lesson in patience and community love; over and over in different ways, elders stressed the importance of working together to respect and protect the water.

As Dr. Manuel Pino points out, the "dendritic patterns of the water ways" mean that the wastes and tailings do not remain contained underground but leak out into the environment, eroding Indigenous people's food sovereignty as game and fish become contaminated over time. For this reason, the Navajo decided in 2005 to refuse to allow any more uranium mining on their lands. As a water-soluble metal, uranium "emits radiation until it stabilizes into lead in 4.5 billion years" (Jim Harding, 2010). Its short-term benefits in terms of energy result in long-term problems, as no one really knows what to do with such long-lived toxic waste.

As one of the conference speakers, Bob Patrick, pointed out, we can't talk about energy without talking about water. As it keeps moving, water connects all forms of life in its ceaseless flow.

Fed freshly hunted caribou and local whitefish, I tasted how delicious the land's provisions are. And I worry about the long-term effects for the Dene people eating wildlife caught in proximity to the uranium mining. What is the relationship between those of us who live in the south and our friends, sisters, brothers, cousins in the north?

the north is hot the ice roads are melting i hold my hand up to
catch some UV rays burn baby burn sings the road's shoulders
this is an inferno of the mining industry's making & the
presumption of consumption the roads follow the mines into
hell hold us hostage with refrigerators computers cell towers
minivans & suvs the everyday paraphernalia of the twenty-first
century in the anthropocene, digging the earth inside out
cracking her bedrock bones for a quick shot of gas to burn, a blip
in the planet's four billion years, little blip with a big footprint
instigating glacial retreat & acidic oceans someone will thank us
for this: the cockroaches who will inherit what's left whether or
not you see the mines you belong to them & they to you we're
not going to shut up, we're water bodies, going to shut down what
has stopped making sense when we could mine landfills richer in
minerals & precious metals than boreal forests, or make biochar

enough: flood out Moloch & ignite the eighth fire

SLEEPLESS IN SOMBA K'E

for the Coney River, otherwise known as the Yellowknife River

precariously perched on once-infinite ice & sweltering in
    broken records
so many degrees of industry intrusion on the front lines of
    global ~~warming~~ dying

along your banks thousands of people speak, sing, shout in
eleven languages & more: Chipewyan, Dogrib, Gwich-in,
North Slavey, South Slavey, Cree, Inuktitut, Inuvialuktun,
Inuinnaqtun, English, French...

illuminated by the midnight sun, you flow regardless of the Giant
Gold Mine's steady leak of 237,000 tonnes of arsenic trioxide,
the bustle of unionized Ekati diamond mine workers, the
repeated dramas of visitors, hunters, bureaucrats, researchers,
tourists, more miners, students

Snap Lake is "Canada's first completely underground diamond
mine." after the unsettlers are finished, what legacy will it leave?

the home of Coney and of Coney-eating Dene for thousands of
years, will this short blip of urban disturbance pass as quickly as
it began, or will it readjust itself to your icy rhythms?

medicines abound as the blind walk & dig: some can hear them,
many can't. what will we learn from crowberry, blueberry,
elderberry, yarrow, caribou, whitefish, Yamozha?

"Water closing over the surface where the rock plunges in."
—Erica Hunt, "Notes for an Oppositional Poetics"

76   sleep replenishes
a tired mind
birdsong renews
wild life in city's midst
ever evolving
under abundant sun
generous rain
a simple breath
again & again
a repeated act
of faith
among
ant crawl
worm squirm
snails & slugs
spider spin
hemlock hold
pigeon coo
baby burble
raccoon scavenge
skunk scamper
antibodies adjust
paramecium propel
salal stretch

"Those who contemplate the beauty of the earth find reserves of strength that will endure as long as life lasts. There is symbolic as well as actual beauty in the migration of birds, the ebb and flow of the tides, the folded bud ready for the spring. There is something infinitely healing in the repeated refrains of nature—the assurance that dawn comes after night, and spring after the winter"
— Rachel Carson, The Sense of Wonder

last year, i never imagined we would be

    round dancing in Glenmore Landing
   round dancing in Chinook Centre
  round dancing in Olympic Plaza
round dancing in Metrotown
round dancing in West Edmonton Mall
 round dancing outside the Cayuga courthouse
  round dancing on Akwesasne
   round dancing on Strombo

  hych'ka!
 mahsi cho!
welalin!
miigwetch!

drumming at Waterfront Station
 drumming at the United Nations
  drumming at Columbia University
  drumming at Granville & Georgia
   drumming at Dalhousie University
  drumming at the Peace Arch
  drumming on Wellington Street
  drumming on Lubicon lands
  drumming in Owen Sound
 drumming in Thunder Bay
  drumming in Somba K'e
 drumming in Chicago
 drumming in Chilliwack
drumming in Kitimat

taking a much needed pause for thought
on tarsands Highway 63
on the 401

on CN rail tracks
with Aamjiwnaang courage
a human river on Ambassador Bridge
time to stop and respect
remember we are all treaty people
unless we live on unceded lands
where ignorant guests can learn to be better ones
by repealing C-45, for starters

we have to stand together in many places all at once
J11, J16, J28
Indigenous spring
Eighth Fire summer
autumn wisdom
winter sleep to
renew Indigenous spring
again & again

it is Gandhi we need to align ourselves with
Gandhi and Gaia and Vandana and Maude *& marbled murrelets &*
    mycorrhizal mats
Winona and Ward and Jaggi and Arundhati *& phytoplankton &*
    peregrine falcons
Naoma and Oren and Toghestiy and Jeannette and Lee &
    bittermelon & bees
Percy and Shiv and Jack and Elizabeth *& chrysanthemum greens &*
    canola, now radiated
Yoko and Yes Men and Chrystos and Dionne *& dolphins & prairie*
    dogs
Theresa and Melina and Pamela and Rosa Parks *& salmon & cedar*
Wab and Harsha and Clayton and Eriel *& eider ducks & water bears*

Takaiya and Roxanna and Glen and David *& wolves & whales*
there is a time for pies and there is a time for rocks *& beavers &*
     snowy plovers
there is a time for poems & a time for rifles *& coral reefs & caribou*   79
there is also a time for the Haudenosaunee Wampum Belt
a time for you
two rivers running side by side
(as long as one party doesn't try to dam, kill the other's river)
and a time for spinning wheels
it is Super Barrio, who stopped 10,000 evictions in Mexico,
     who i look to
it is the Zapatistas, the Mohawks, the KI, the Lhe Lin Liyin
the Mother Earth Water Walkers, the 20-year-olds suddenly in
     Parliament, the grannies & the grandkids
it is the children i will never see, but who i hope will live and
     drink clean, wild water

*with gratitude to Chief Theresa Spence and Idle No More for participatory
leadership in the service of lands, waters & all living beings*

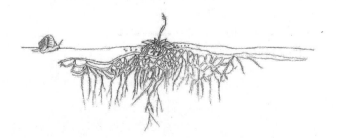

80   the women hold space like trees do, sweet fresh air between
their tender branches. unseen roots draw deep down into dark
moist sustenance, making homes for songbirds, windsong and
children who puff with asthmatic exertion. the women stand in
front of army trucks & policemen, uniforms & riot gear with
only their soft skin & clear eyes to protect their beating hearts.
the mothers, the sisters, the aunties, the grannies, the daughters
crack open the ugly pavement of unjust laws & find old rivers
underneath. quietly, firmly, they pray & burn offerings for the
four directions to come together in sacred commitment to all of
creation: the frogs, the slugs, the hummingbirds, the whales, the
mountains, the creeks, the laughing ones & the crying ones, the
tough ones & the weak ones, the silly ones & the serious ones,
the clowns & the cooks, the farmers & the fishers. the women dig
their toes into the generous earth remembering their mothers
and their neighbours, their relatives who fly and those who
swim. the women have forgotten so much but they are starting
to remember. no matter how many of them have been killed,
beaten, insulted, the women continue to stand together. the
women plant trees & gardens. the women eat fresh peaches &
can huckleberries. they compost & compile recipes. the women
forage for mushrooms & cultivate stubborn corn. they praise the
sun & the night with their toil. they tickle each other and guffaw.
the women lick their lips with gusto. they perch on the edge of
teetering cities. they jump into organic fields. the women build
homes with their beloveds. the women find ways to laugh even
when life isn't funny. the women remain

References & Influences

Abuela Grillo. http://vimeo.com/13195764

Armstrong, Christopher, Matthew Evenden and H.V. Nelles. *The River Returns: An Environmental History of the Bow.* Montreal: McGill-Queen's University Press, 2009.

"Arsenic Trioxide and the Frozen Block Method." Aboriginal Affairs and Northern Development Canada. http://www.aadnc-aandc.gc.ca/eng/1100100027422/1100100027423

Athabasca Chipewyan First Nation. http://www.acfn.com/

Berland, Jody. "Walkerton: The Memory of Matter," *Topia* 14 (Fall 2005): 93-108.

"Bernie Krause discusses biophony and music with Sir George Martin" from *Rhythms of Life. BBC.* 9 May 2012. https://www.youtube.com/watch?v=feexRcCHh3k

Bing Ai. Dir. Yan Feng. 2007.

Bocking, Richard. *Mighty River: A Portrait of the Fraser.* Vancouver: Douglas & McIntyre, 1997.

Boyd, Andrew. *Beautiful Trouble: A Toolbox for Revolution.* OR Books, 2013. http://beautifultrouble.org/

Bow River Basin Council. http://wsow.brbc.ab.ca/

Cardinal, Jesse. "The Tar Sands Healing Walk." *A Line in the Tar Sands.* Eds. Toban Black et al. Toronto: Between the Lines, 2014.

Carson, Rachel. *The Sea Around Us.* Toronto: Oxford University Press, 1991.

---. *The Sense of Wonder.* New York: Harper, 1998.

Cole, Peter, et al. *Speaking for Ourselves: Environmental Justice in Canada.* Vancouver: University of British Columbia Press, 2009.

Cycle to the Sacred. Beyond Boarding. Summer 2014. http://www.beyondboarding.org/cycle-to-the-sacred

Dai Qing, qtd. in William Wan, "Amid severe drought, the Chinese government admits mistakes with the Three Gorges Dam," *Washington Post*, 4 June 2011. http://www.washingtonpost.com/world/asia-pacific/chinese-government-confronts-reality-of-three-gorges-dam-mistakes/2011/05/30/AGfXx0IH_story.html

De Beers. https://www.canada.debeersgroup.com/Mining/

D'Souza, Radha. Presentation at Keepers of the Water. Lac Brochet, Manitoba. 2011.

Evaluation of Four Reports on Contamination of the Athabasca River System by Oil Sands Operations. 2011. http://environment.alberta.ca/documents/wmdrc_-_final_report_march_7_2011.pdf

False Creek Watershed Society. http://www.falsecreekwatershed.org/

Feld, Steven. "From Ethnomusicology to Echo-Muse-Ecology." *Acoustic Ecology.* 2001. http://www.acousticecology.org/writings/echomuseecology.html

First Voices. http://www.firstvoices.com

Gabrielle-Pape, Jada, of the Saanich and Snuneymuxw Nations. Artist talk, 17 Sept 2013.

George, Chief Dan. "Words to a Grandchild." *Native Poetry in Canada.* Eds. Jeannette Armstrong and Lally Grauer. Peterborough, ON: Broadview Press, 2001.

Goldstick, Miles. *Wollaston.* Montreal: Black Rose Books, 1987.

Harding, Jim. "Proposed Uranium Mine Wouldn't Get Go-Ahead in South." *No Nukes: Go Renewable Canada.* 5 Sept. 2010. http://crowsnestecology.wordpress.com/2010/09/05/proposed-uranium-mine-wouldn%E2%80%99t-get-go-ahead-in-south/

Hillman, Brenda. "Hydrology of California: An Ecopoetical Statement." *Practical Water.* Middletown, CT: Wesleyan, 2009.

Hix, Harvey, ed. *Ley Lines.* Waterloo, ON: Wilfrid Laurier UP, 2014.

Hume, Stephen. *A Walk with the Rainy Sisters.* Madeira Park, BC: Harbour, 2010.

Hunt, Erica. "Notes for an Oppositional Poetics." *Moving Borders: Three Decades of Innovative Writing by Women.* Ed. Mary Margaret Sloan. Jersey City, NJ: Talisman House, 680-87.

I Ching Online. http://www.ichingonline.net.

Irland, Basia. *Water Library.* Albuquerque: University of New Mexico Press, 2007.

Jaremko, Gordon. "Pipeline to the Pacific." 3 Nov 2007. http://www.canada. com/edmontonjournal/news/business/story.html?id=31c8d460-da17-4d52-af2b-a3b134b5c905&k=58903.

Keepers of the Water. http://keepersofthewater.ca/

Kinder Morgan. "TMX – Anchor Loop Project Frequently Asked Questions." http://www.kindermorgan.com/business/canada/tmx_documentation/FAQ_v7.doc

Kino-nda-niimi Collective, eds. *The Winter We Danced: Voices from the Past, the Future, and the Idle No More Movement.* Winnipeg: ARP Books, 2014.

Klein, Naomi. *This Changes Everything: Capitalism vs. the Climate.* Toronto: Alfred Knopf, 2014.

Laboucan Massimo, Melina, qtd in Nobel Women's Initiative. 28 Nov. 2012. http://nobelwomensinitiative.org/2012/11/day-4-spotlighting-melina-laboucan-massimo-lubicon-lake-cree-nation-canada/

Land Is Life: Indigenous Defenders Speak. Featuring Ancestral Pride - Gwaiina and Xhopakelxhit sovereign Ahoushat / Snuneymuxw, Mel Bazil of the Wet'suwet'en and Gitxsan, Jackson Crick of the Tsilhqot'in Nation, Freda Huson - spokesperson of the Unist'ot'en clan of the Wet'suwet'en, Arthur Manuel of the Secwepemc Nation, Kanahus Pelkey of the Secwepemc Nation, Khelsilem Rivers - Skwxwu7mesh-Kwakwaka'wakw, and Toghestiy of the Wet'suwet'en nation. 16 Dec. 2013. https://www. youtube.com/watch?v=iamLYN8CVBQ

Leal, Teresa. In *Environmental Justice Reader.* Eds. Joni Adamson et al. Tucson, AZ, University of Arizona Press, 2002.

Leclerc, Christine et al. *Enpipeline.* Smithers, BC: Creekstone Press, 2012.

Lee, Bruce. Interview by Pierre Berton. *The Pierre Berton Show.* Dec 9, 1971. Youtube.

Lilburn, Tim. *Living in the World As If It Were Home.* Toronto: Cormorant Books, 2002.

Maathai, Wangari. *Taking Root.* http://takingrootfilm.com/

84   MacEwan, Grant. *Watershed: Reflections on Water.* Edmonton: NeWest Press, 2000.

Maracle, Lee. "Water," forthcoming in *Downstream: Reimagining Water.* Wilfrid Laurier University Press.

McAllister, Angus. *Life Cycle: Sustaining the Story of Water in BC.* 19 Nov. 2012. https://www.freshwateralliance.ca/sites/default/files/resources/bc_freshwater_focus_groups_report.pdf

McKibben, Bill. "A World That Works." *Written in Water.* Ed. Irena Salina. Washington, DC: National Geographic, 2010. 101–106.

McMenamin, Mark and Dianna McMenamin. *Hypersea: Life on Land.* New York: Columbia University Press, 1994.

Merton, Thomas. "Rain and the Rhinoceros." *Raids on the Unspeakable.* New York: New Directions, 1966. 9–23.

Mining Watch. http://www.miningwatch.ca/after-mine-0

Mitchell, Alanna. *Sea Sick: The Global Ocean in Crisis.* Toronto: Emblem, 2010.

Moore, Charles. *Plastic Ocean.* New York: Avery, 2011.

Mottainai. http://mottainai.info/english/

Nahanee, Amanda. "Aboriginal Perspectives on Climate Change." https://www.youtube.com/watch?v=OwH_0jXYOQU

Neimanis, Astrida. "We Are All Bodies of Water." *Water.* Ed. John Knechtel. Cambridge, MA: MIT Press, 82-91.

Nikiforuk, Andrew. *Tar Sands.* Vancouver: Greystone Books, 2008.

Pasteur, Louis, qtd in Jessica Sachs. *Good Germs, Bad Germs.* New York: Hill and Wang, 2007.

Paulette, Francois, qtd in "Indigenous Peoples of Canada March on Canadian Embassy in Copenhagen to Protest Tar Sands." *Democracy Now.*

15 Dec. 2009. http://www.democracynow.org/2009/12/15/indigenous_
peoples_of_canada_march_on

Plath, Sylvia. "The Beekeeper's Daughter." *Sylvia Plath: The Collected Poems.* Ed.
Ted Hughes. New York: HarperPerennial, 2008. 118.

Rights and Responsibilities: A short film featuring Toghestiy and Mel Bazil. Beyond Boarding.
9 July 2014. http://vimeo.com/99574930

Roy, Arundhati. "Another World Is Not Only Possible, She Is on Her Way."
Truthout. 18 April 2014. Web.

Royte, Elizabeth. *Garbage Land: On the Secret Trail of Trash.* New York: Back Bay
Books, 2006.

Samaqan: Water Stories. APTN. http://www.samaqan.ca/

Sandford, Robert. *Restoring the Flow: Confronting the World's Water Woes.* Victoria, BC:
Rocky Mountain Books, 2011.

Seglins, Dave. "G20 report slams police for 'excessive' force." CBC. 16 May
2012. http://www.cbc.ca/news/canada/g20-report-slams-police-for-
excessive-force-1.1137051

Simpson, Leanne. "Restoring Nationhood: Addressing Land Dispossession
in the Canadian Reconciliation Discourse." 13 Nov. 2013. http://www.
sfu.ca/tlcvan/clients/sfu_woodwards/2013-11-13_Woodwards_VOCE_
Restoring_Nationhood_12308/

Solnit, Rebecca. "Revolution of the Snails." TomDispatch.com. 15 Jan.
2008. http://www.tomdispatch.com/post/174881

Soros, George, qtd in David Suzuki and Holly Dressel. *Good News for a Change:
How Everyday People Are Helping the Planet.* Vancouver: Greystone Books, 2002.
41.

South March Highlands website. http://www.southmarchhighlands.ca/

Steingraber, Sandra. *Living Downstream.* New York: Vintage, 1998.

Tar Sands Healing Walk. http://www.healingwalk.org/

A Terrible Beauty: Edward Burtynsky. Vancouver Art Gallery. May 2014.

Teztan Biny: The Fight for Fish Lake. http://www.raventrust.com/
fishlaketeztanbiny.html

Village of Widows. http://lindumfilms.com/villageofwidows

Wah, Fred. "High Muck a Muck: Playing Chinese, An Interactive Poem." http://highmuckamuck.ca/

Waking the Green Tiger. http://www.facetofacemedia.ca/page.php?sectionID=2

Wallace, David Foster. *This Is Water,* reprinted as "Plain old untrendy troubles and emotions." *The Guardian.* 20 Sept. 2008. http://www.theguardian. com/books/2008/sep/20/fiction

Walia, Harsha. *Undoing Border Imperialism.* Oakland, CA: AK Press, 2013.

Warshall, Peter. *Septic Tank Practices.* New York: Doubleday, 1979.

Weber, Bob. "Native leader asks James Cameron to back fight against oilsands." *Toronto Star.* 28 Sept 2010. http://www.thestar.com/news/ canada/2010/09/28/native_leader_asks_james_cameron_to_back_fight_ against_oilsands.html#

Whitehead, Jerry. Artist talk. 17 Sept 2013.

Wolf, Aaron, et al. "Peace in the Pipeline." BBC News. 13 Feb 2009. <http:// news.bbc.co.uk/2/hi/science/nature/7886646.stm>.

Wyss, Cease. *Indigenous Plant Diva,* dir. Kamala Todd, National Film Board, 2008, http://www.cultureunplugged.com/documentary/watch-online/ play/2819/Indigenous-Plant-Diva

Yeats, W.B. "Easter 1916," from *The Collected Poems of W.B. Yeats,* via www.poetryfoundation.org

EPILOGUE: LETTER SENT BACK IN TIME
FROM 2115

here is wonder, despite armies of mistakes. darshan. the heavens still circle us, & we them. from ovum to star orbits, rebalance begins, practical & spiritual. in the great return, toilets don't flush; they compost. people cease & desist from desecrating water by pissing & shitting in it. other ways to move waste, besides water, prevail. we live in the world as if it were our only home, loving dreamtime & full breath. spontaneous compassion sprouts in the cracks of collapsing systems. as the rampant destruction of drinkable water finally stops, mutual-aid lifeboats emerge. seui dihk sehk chyun. gradual & magical, the syntax of hope percolates into bathrooms & basements, glistens in alleyways turned arbours. city dwellers cultivate gentle water, in the shape of sturdy kale, crisp apples, airy chicken coops. ubuntu. glimpse elders in every school, children in every seniors' home. organic gardens spread through public grounds, healing lodges & neighbourhoods. treaties mature, deepening respect like old-growth roots. springwater protection, fogcatchers, cedar, all thicken, as does birdsong with the return of habitat & empathy. three sisters sing louder in our guts & muscles. we learn the languages of roots & fungus medicines. dandelion, yarrow, burdock, lingzhi. everyone slows, attends to the waxing & waning moon each lunar cycle. balance quietly returns to the commons, as the solace of night matches the solar feed-in tariffs by day. the sun meets the power of the moon. serious play enters work in a big way. nobody is the boss of anybody but themselves. hemp mostly takes plastic's place. through cob construction, occupations of empty condos & community sweat equity, everyone who wants a home, has one. indigenous resurgence slows climate instability & deflates apocalyptic fervor. today people live & watch water's journey the way they used to watch the dow jones, as the flow of tao reaffirms ocean life. hych'ka.

水滴石穿

Acknowledgements

It is an enormous gift and a humbling responsibility to live on the beautiful, unceded Coast Salish homelands of the Tsleil-Waututh (Burrard), XwMuthkwium (Musqueam), Skwxuwu-7mesh (Squamish) and Stó:lō Nations. I dedicate this book to all the Keepers of the Water, and to restitution for Indigenous peoples. As an (un)settler whose ancestors hail from the Pearl River delta, I vow to do my part to support climate justice and to foster respectful co-existence with land, water and life.

Thanks to Dorothy for asking: "Can you love the land like I do?"

Gratitude to the many who make poetry possible:

Kindred spirits Larissa Lai, Hiromi Goto, Dorothy Christian, Shahira Sakiyama. Keeper of cultural memory and integrity: Lee Maracle. Artists: Marika Swan, Cindy Mochizuki. Careful readers: Kateri Akiwenzie-Damm, Wang Ping, Fred Wah, Roy Miki, Larissa, and Hiromi (thank you for late-hour fast response!). Thanks to ET for rapid character assistance. Shout out to poet-organizers Christine Leclerc and Steve Collis. Family village: Cindy, Luke, Lana, Jeff, Pat, Billie, Canace, Peter, Cedar, Soleil, Zee, Cary, Sae, Koji, Tania, Miranda, Ming, Mariza, Daphne, Ping, See, Lawrence, Teresa, Thomas, Herman, Tammy, Holly, and more from the Wong and Chan clans and beyond. Love plus water makes Walter.

Steadfast spirits and encouraging travelers along the journey: Cecilia (knitter, walker, impromptu organizer extraordinaire), Janice (generous host and tireless truth-teller), Bao, Jamila, Lily, Sid, Jordan, Alannah, Denise, Elisa, Baco, Jamie, Eric, Michelle, Weyman, Jeff, Joah, Brett, Donna, Agnes, Shauna, Karen, Jo-Anne, Mimi, Peg, Daphne, Henry, Rain, Kelly, Chelsey and the creative witness group. Rainway & underground streams crew: Shahira, Dan, Bryn, Amy, Max, Sarah, Sara, Greta,

Bruce, Naomi, Melanie, Rodney, Choo, Celia, Michael. Keepers of the Water and the Athabasca: Sam, Jesse, Harvey, Bruce, Helene, Julie, Janice, Evelyn, Nancy, Harvey, Bob, Caleb and more. All the Downstream workshop participants—you know who you are—and helpers/supporters: Dorothy, Larissa, Walter, Karolle, Alex, Peter, Pat, Karen, Matthew, Jeneen, Samantha, Vanessa, Choo, Michelle, Brenda, Elisas, Astrida, Janine. Book magicians: Silas White and Carleton Wilson. Gratitude to the caretakers, organizers, poets, scientists, sacred firekeepers of Burnaby Mountain, and to the protectors of Cəsnaʔəm:.

I raise my hands in appreciation and thanks to the guardians who inspire us to remember our human responsibilities to take care of the land, the earth, the waters, for past, present and future generations: the Unist'ot'en Camp, the Tsleil Waututh Sacred Trust, the signatories of the Save the Fraser Declaration, the Klabona Keepers, the Hupacasath, the Healing Walk organizers, the Athabasca Chipewyan First Nation, the Mikisew Cree, the Mother Earth Water Walkers, the Haudenosaunee at Kanehsatake and Kahnawake, the water protectors at Elsipogtog, the Peace and Dignity Journey, and many more protectors and defenders than I can possibly name here, from Pacific to Atlantic, Arctic to Equator, inspiring in courage and heart. In Indigenous resurgence and respect for spirit of place, I see hope for humanity. Over the years, forums organized by No One Is Illegal and Rising Tide have offered much needed education.

I would like to acknowledge the support of the Social Sciences and Humanities Research Council of Canada for the research-creation project and workshop, *Downstream: A Poetics of Water*, hosted at Emily Carr University of Art and Design. In addition to the *Downstream* workshop, many gatherings and events fed my soul and this manuscript, including, but not only: the Keepers of the Water Gatherings in Cold Lake, Fort Nelson, Lac Brochet, Hatchet Lake (and earlier gatherings that remind us "Water is boss"); Encuentro in Montreal (thanks to the Canadian Consortium on Performance and Politics in the Americas); First Nations and Chinese Elders Meet and Greet in the Downtown Eastside; the Activating the Heart: Storytelling, Knowledge and Relationship Workshop in Yellowknife; the Thinking with Water workshop at Concordia University; the Tragedy of the Market Conference: from Crisis to Commons, (Re)Scriptae: the University of Calgary English Honours Symposium; the World Humanities Symposium at Simon Fraser University; SFU's Lunch Poems; the Green Words, Green Worlds Conference at York University; the Material Cultures conference at the University of Ottawa; the Cross-Pollinations Workshop at the University of Alberta; the Under Western Skies Conference at Mount Royal University; the conferences organized by the Association for Literature, Environment and Culture in Canada Conference (ALECC) and the Association for the Study of Literature and the Environment (ASLE); and more. Much-needed sabbatical time from Emily Carr, spent in Miami, also helped nourish this manuscript.

Close to home, the Rainway conversations, design workshops, community parades, street mural painting along St. George St., storytellers' bench at the headwaters of the buried creek te Statləw, neighbourhood festivals, and block parties, are encouraging signs of life. Shout out to neighbourhood hubs – Rhizome, now Heartwood. Many brothers and sisters at the Federation of Post-Secondary Educators—including my colleagues at the Emily Carr Faculty Association (Local 22)—have also taught me a lot about the value of solidarity and collegial communication.

Poems in this book have previously appeared in various forms in the following publications: *The Winter We Danced: Voices from the Past, the Future, and the Idle No More Movement*; *Decolonization: Indigeneity, Education and Society*; *Women and Environments International Magazine*; the press release chapbook *r/ally*; *The Enpipe Line: 70,000 km of poetry written in resistance to the Northern Gateway pipeline proposal*; *Capitalism Nature Socialism*; *Poetry Is Dead* (commissioned in response to

Edward Burtynsky's exhibition, *A Terrible Beauty*, at the Vancouver Art Gallery); *Ricepaper*; *Canadian Literature*; *A Verse Map of Vancouver*; *West Coast Line* (with thanks to Steve Collis for commune collaboration); *Interim*; *Eleven Eleven*; *Eighteen Bridges*; *Ley Lines*; *Canada and Beyond: A Journal of Canadian Literary and Cultural Studies*; *Force Field: 77 Women Poets of British Columbia*; and the forthcoming anthologies *Alone Together*, *Activating the Heart* and *Make It True*.

Relevant prose has appeared in the *Thinking with Water* anthology, *rabble.ca*, *Common Ground*, *Feminist Review*, the *Dominion*, *Journal of Chinese Philosophy*, *The Capilano Review*, *Salish Seas: An Anthology of Text + Image*, *Cultivating Canada: Reconciliation Through the Lens of Cultural Diversity*, *Alternatives: Environmental Ideas and Action*, *The Goose*, *Canadian Literature*, *Front magazine* and *Active Geographies: Women & Struggles on the Left Coast* (*West Coast Line* 58).

Any inadvertent omissions are a symptom of overwork and the need for a more humane economy.

PHOTOGRAPH ON PAGE 55:
Chinese immigrants on the deck of the "Black Diamond" (sailing vessel, BC). c 1889, Library and Archives Canada 1973-050.

PHOTO CREDIT: JANE SLEMON

ABOUT THE AUTHOR

Rita Wong is the author of three books of poetry: *monkeypuzzle* (Press Gang, 1998), *forage* (Nightwood Editions, 2007) and *sybil unrest* (Line Books, 2008, with Larissa Lai). *forage* was the winner of the 2008 Dorothy Livesay Poetry Prize and Canada Reads Poetry 2011. Wong is an associate professor in the Faculty of Culture and Community at the Emily Carr University of Art and Design on the unceded Coast Salish territories also known as Vancouver.

I come from a whaling community on the west coast of Vancouver Island in the heart of well-known Clayoquot Sound. I was born on the beach in the place where our people used to bring the whales in. When our people were whaling, they prepared their whole lives spiritually to be worthy of a gift as generous as a whale. Everyone in the community had to work in unity to ensure the hunt was safe and successful. Each whale was such a bountiful offering of food for the community and each part of the whale was utilized and celebrated.

As a Tla-o-qui-aht woman there are many gifts I am hoping to bring home to my community, and I understand that I am on a spiritual journey to lay the groundwork so that I am ready when they arrive. Pook-mis, the drowned whaler, lies at the bottom of the sea floor and offers a warning that things can go horribly wrong if you are not properly prepared.

Becoming Worthy is a part of a series of woodblock prints exploring my people's natural and supernatural relationship with whales. Further prints in the series can be seen on my website marikaswan.com.